The Ultimate Self-Teaching Method! Songbook

Play Mandolin Today! Songbook

Featuring 10 Pop & Folk Favorites!

PLAYBACK+
Speed • Pitch • Balance • Loop

To access audio visit:
www.halleonard.com/mylibrary

Enter Code
3636-6752-9526-6116

Mandolin, all backing instruments and arrangements by Douglas Baldwin except "My Heart Will Go On" (Taylor Baldwin, oboe and percussion; Nicole Soder, violins; and Max Hanks, cellos) and "I Hope You Dance" (Nicole Sodor, violin; Max Hanks, cello; Taylor Baldwin, percussion)

All tracks recorded at Coyote Music Studio, Saint James, NY

ISBN 978-1-4803-1286-9

HAL•LEONARD®
CORPORATION

7777 W. BLUEMOUND RD. P.O. BOX 13819 MILWAUKEE, WI 53213

Visit Hal Leonard Online at
www.halleonard.com

Introduction

Welcome to the *Play Mandolin Today! Songbook*. This book includes a mix of well-known pop and folk favorites, and is intended for the beginning to intermediate player. It can be used on its own, or as a supplement to the *Play Mandolin Today!* method series.

Contents

About the Audio

Online access to full-band demo recordings of every song in this book is included, so you can hear how they sound and then play along with the provided play-along track when you're ready. A tuning track is also provided to help you tune your instrument by ear.

To access the audio for download or streaming, visit **www.halleonard.com/mylibrary** and enter the code found at the front of this book.

Now including PLAYBACK+, a multi-functional audio player that allows you to slow down audio without changing pitch, set loop points, and more—available exclusively from Hal Leonard.

Song Structure

Most songs have different sections that might be recognizable by any or all of the following:

- **Introduction** (or "Intro"): This is a short section at the beginning that "introduces" the song to the listeners.

- **Verses**: One of the main sections of the song—the part that includes most of the storyline—is the *verse*. There will usually be several verses, all with the same music but each with different lyrics.

- **Chorus**: Perhaps the most memorable section of the song is the *chorus*. Again, there might be several choruses, but each chorus will often have the same lyrics and music.

- **Bridge**: This section makes a transition from one part of a song to the next. For example, you may find a bridge between the chorus and next verse.

- **Outro**: Similar to the "intro," this section brings the song to an end.

Lyrics

Lyrics to all of the great songs in this book are included. They are shown below the staff as a guide to help you keep your place in the music.

Fermata ⌢

This symbol tells you to hold the note(s) longer than the normal time value. You will often see a fermata at the end of a song over the final note or chord.

Repeats & Endings

Repeat signs ‖: :‖ tell you to repeat everything in between them. If only one sign appears :‖ , repeat from the beginning of the piece.

First and Second Endings

Play the song through to the first ending, repeat back to the first repeat sign, or beginning of the song (whichever is the case). Play through the song again, but skip the first ending and play the second ending.

D.S. al Coda

When you see these words, go back and repeat from this symbol: 𝄋

Play until you see the words "To Coda," then skip to the Coda, indicated by this symbol: ⊕

Now just finish the song.

Sixteenth-Note Rhythms

A **sixteenth note** lasts half as long as an eighth note—a quarter of a beat—and is written with two flags or two beams. There are four sixteenth notes in one beat. To play sixteenths it helps to count: "one-e-and-a, two-e-and-a, three-e-and-a, four-e-and-a."

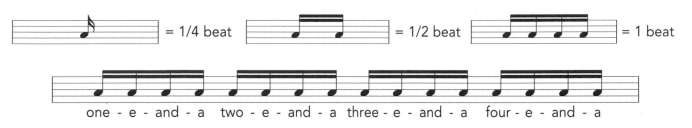

This is what it looks like when eighth notes and sixteenths are mixed in the same beat. The counting is the same, except for one silent sixteenth (in parentheses).

Triplet Rhythms

A **triplet** is a group of three notes played in the space of two. Whereas eighth notes divide a beat (quarter note) into two parts, **eighth-note triplets** divide one beat into three equal parts. To count this rhythm, it helps to say the word "tri-pl-et" with each syllable spaced evenly over the length of one beat.

Other Time Signatures

All song examples presented in the *Play Mandolin Today!* Level One method book have been in the two most common meters: 4/4 and 3/4. Here are two other meters that appear in this song book.

2/4 Time

Time signatures tell the player two things: the top number tells how many beats there are in a measure of music, and the bottom number tells what kind of note equals one beat. That means in 2/4 time, there are two beats per measure and a quarter note equals one beat.

6/8 Time

Using the same formula described above, 6/8 time tells us that there are six beats per measure and the eighth note equals one beat. In other words, there are six eighth notes per measure.

Blue Moon of Kentucky

Words and Music by Bill Monroe

Intro
Moderately

Chorus

Blue moon of Ken - tuck - y keep on shin - ing. Shine on the one that's

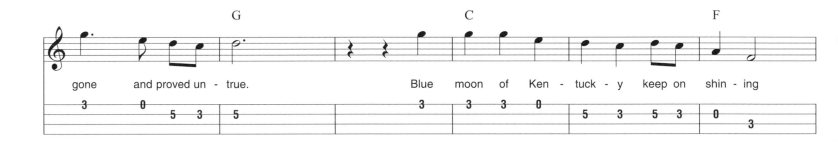

gone and proved un - true. Blue moon of Ken - tuck - y keep on shin - ing

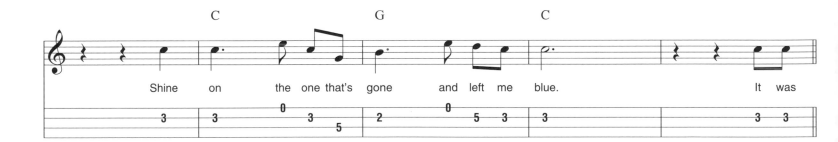

Shine on the one that's gone and left me blue. It was

Bridge

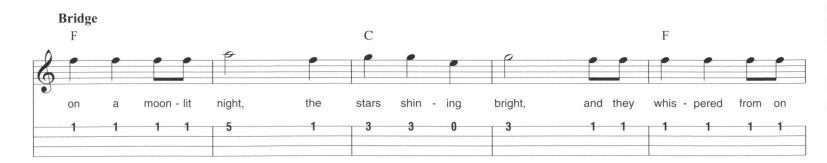

on a moon - lit night, the stars shin - ing bright, and they whis - pered from on

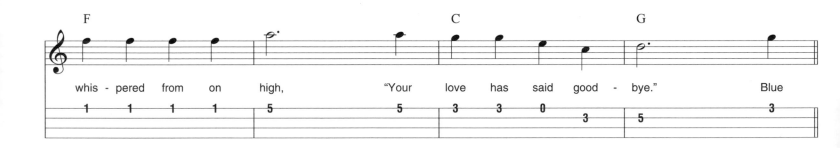

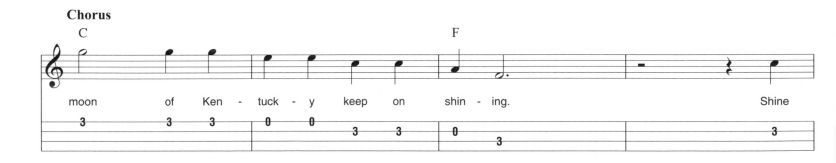

My Heart Will Go On

(Love Theme From 'Titanic')

from the Paramount and Twentieth Century Fox Motion Picture TITANIC
Music by James Horner
Lyric by Will Jennings

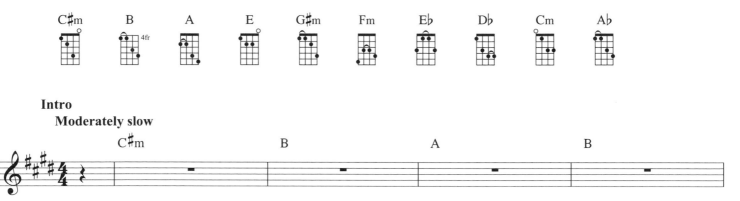

Intro
Moderately slow

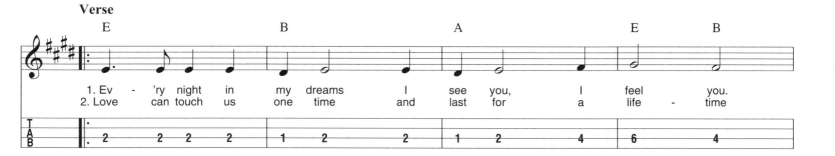

Verse

1. Ev - 'ry night in my dreams I see you, I feel you.
2. Love can touch us one time and last for a life - time

That is how I know you go on.
and nev - er let go till we're gone.

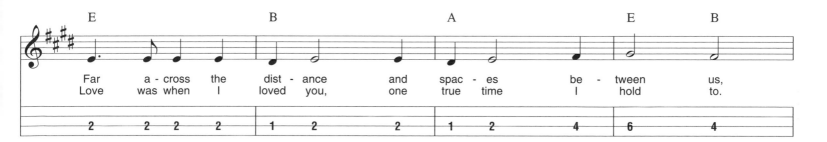

Far a - cross the dist - ance and spac - es be - tween us,
Love was when I loved you, one true time I hold to.

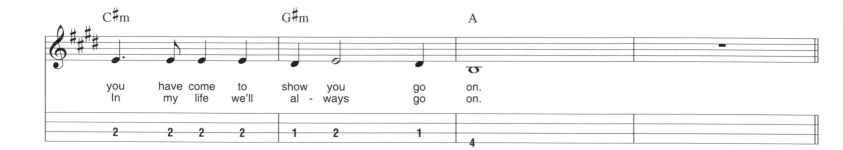

you have come to show you go on.
In my life we'll al - ways go on.

Chorus

Near, far, where - ev - er you are I be -

lieve that the heart does go on. _____

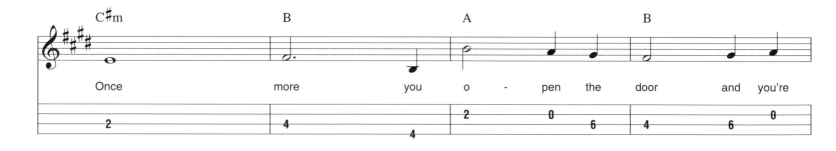

Once more you o - pen the door and you're

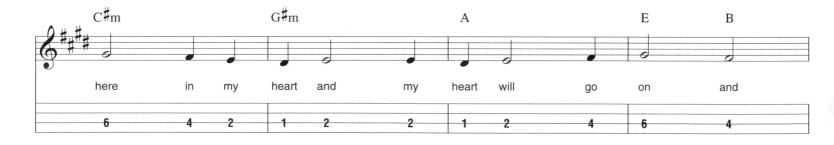

here in my heart and my heart will go on and

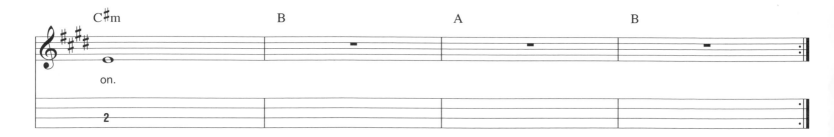

on.

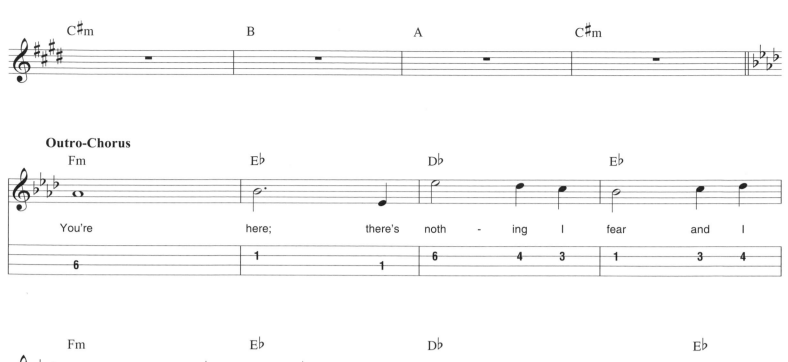

Outro-Chorus

You're here; there's noth - ing I fear and I

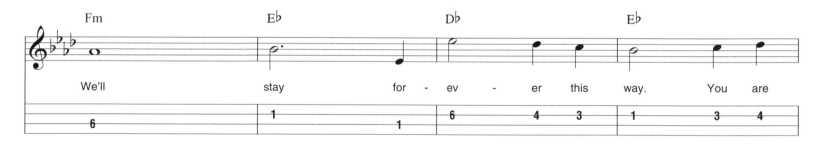

know that my heart will go on. _____

We'll stay for - ev - er this way. You are

safe in my heart and my heart will go on and

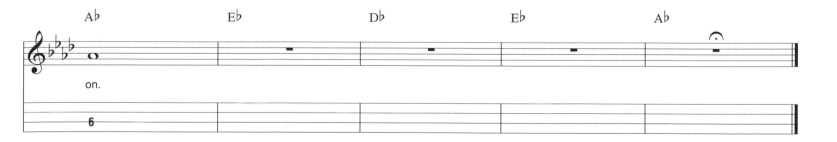

on.

Dark Eyes

Russian Cabaret Song

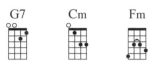

Intro
Moderately slow

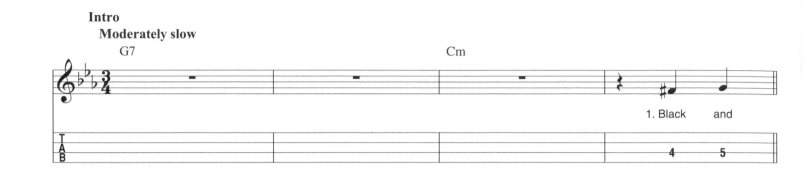

1. Black   and

Verse

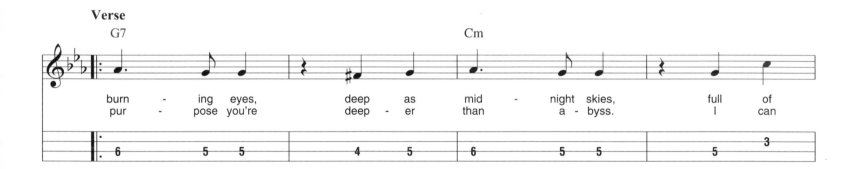

burn - ing eyes,   deep as mid - night skies,   full of
pur - pose you're   deep - er than   night a - byss.   I can

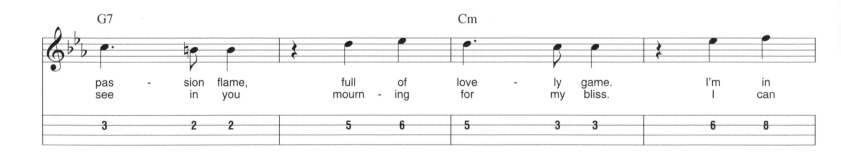

pas - sion flame,   full of love - ly game.   I'm in
see in you   mourn - ing love for   my bliss.   I can

love   with you,   I'm a - fraid   of you.   Days when
see   in you   that tri - umph - al flame   where my

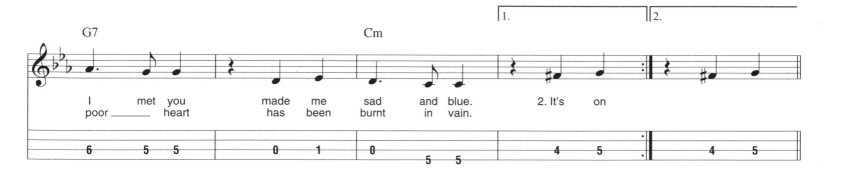

I _____ met you _____ made me sad and blue. 2. It's on

poor _____ heart _____ has been burnt in vain.

Interlude

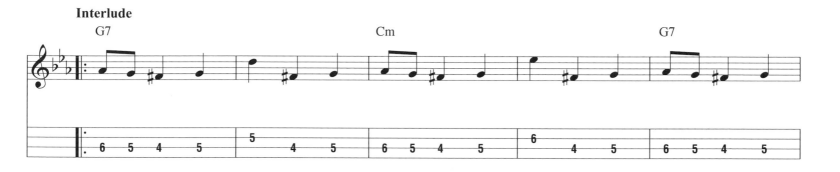

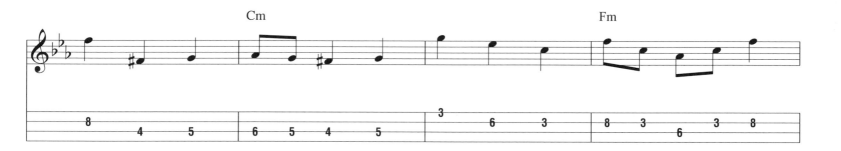

rit.

Jolene

Words and Music by Dolly Parton

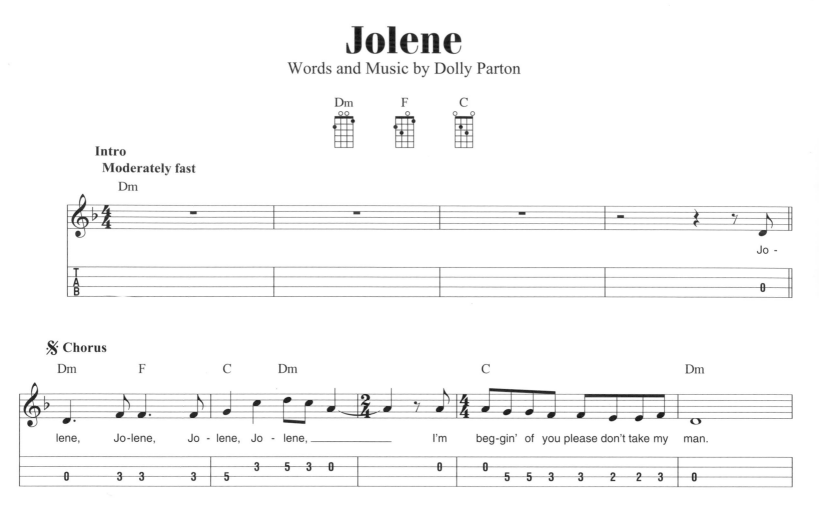

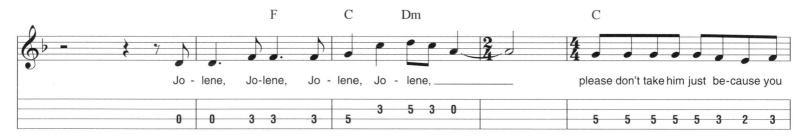

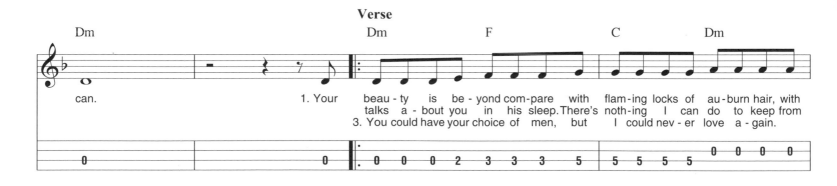

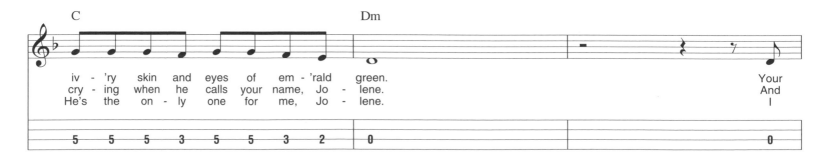

Never on Sunday

Words by Billy Towne
Music by Manos Hadjidakis

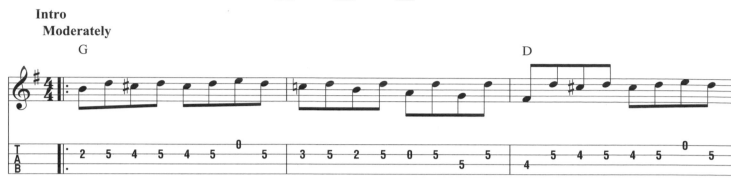

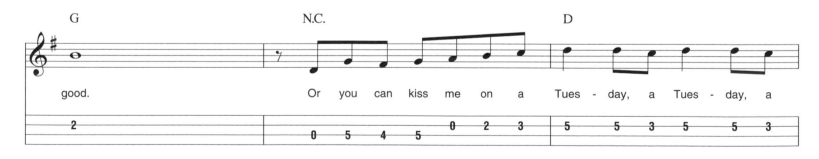

Wednes-day, a Thurs-day, a Fri-day and Sat-ur-day's the best. But nev-er, nev-er on a

Sun-day, a Sun-day, a Sun-day 'cause that's my day of rest. Most an-y

Chorus

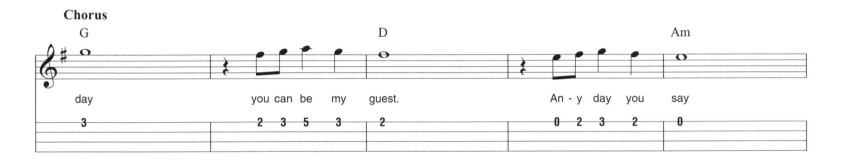

day you can be my guest. An-y day you say

but my day of rest. Just name the day

that you like the best, on-ly stay a-way

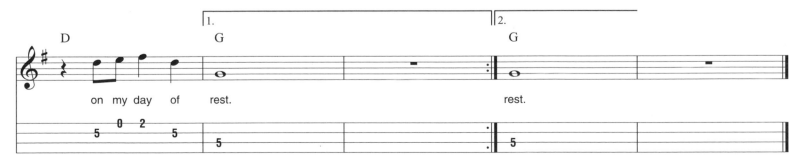

on my day of rest. rest.

I Hope You Dance

Words and Music by Tia Sillers and Mark D. Sanders

The Sound of Silence

Words and Music by Paul Simon

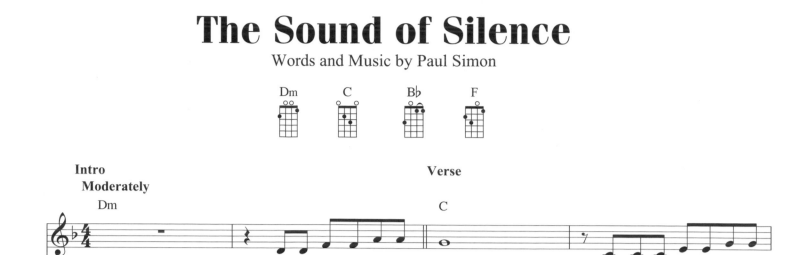

Intro
Moderately

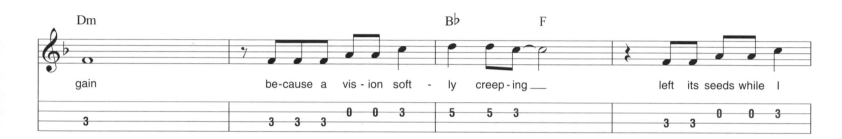

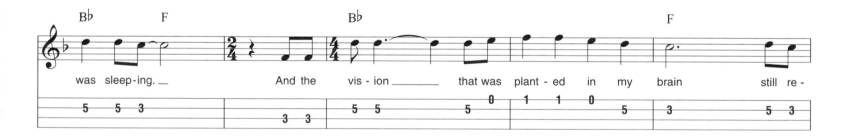

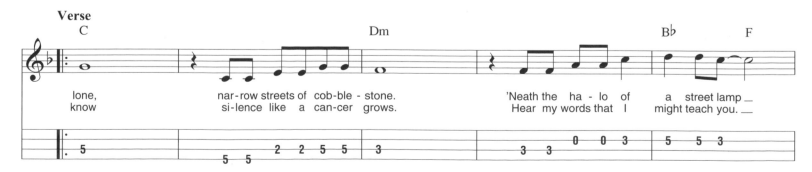

With or Without You

Words and Music by U2

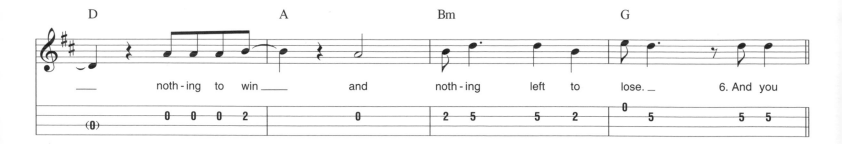

Verse

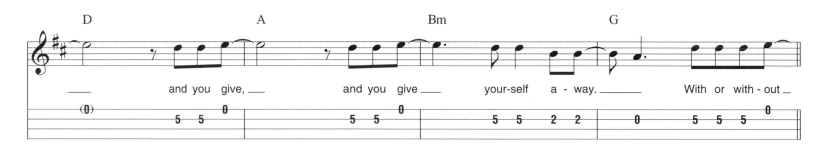

Chorus

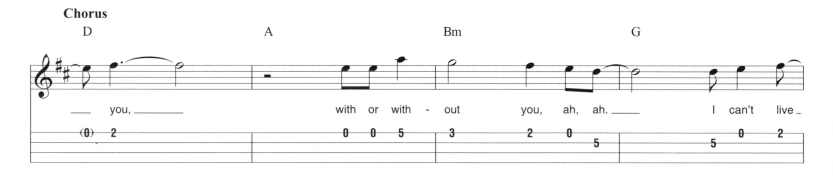

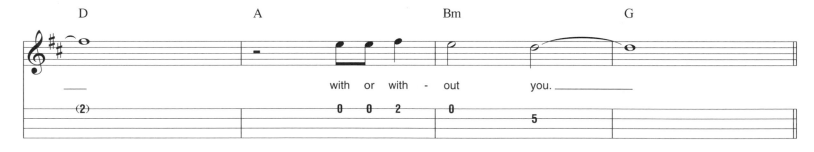

Bridge

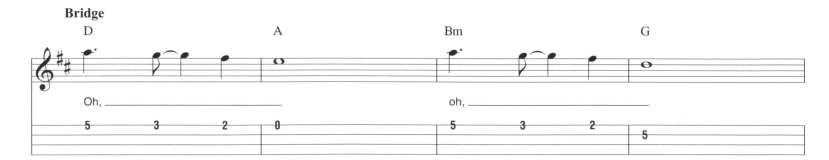

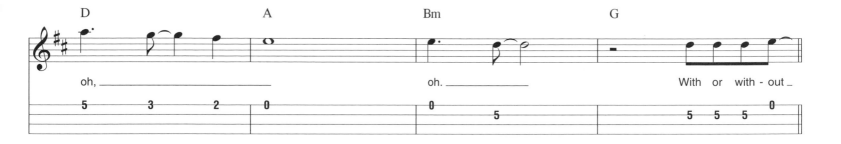

Chorus

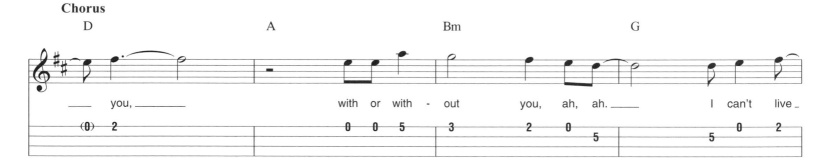

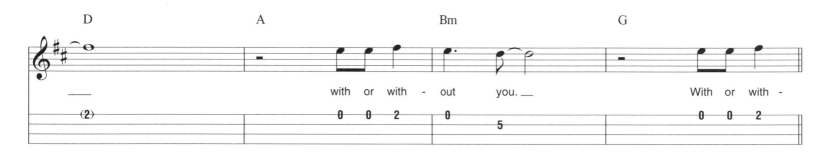

Outro

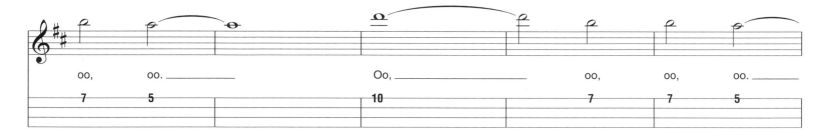

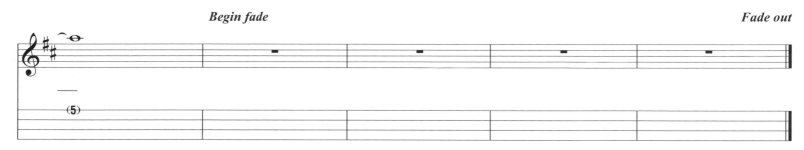

The Kesh Jig

Traditional Irish

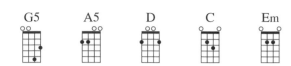

Intro
Moderately

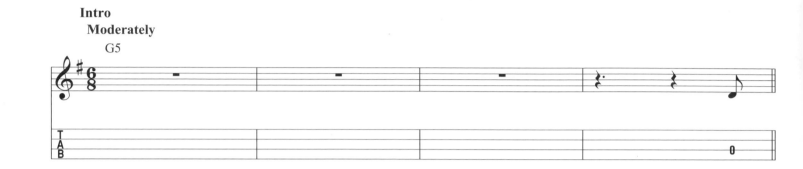

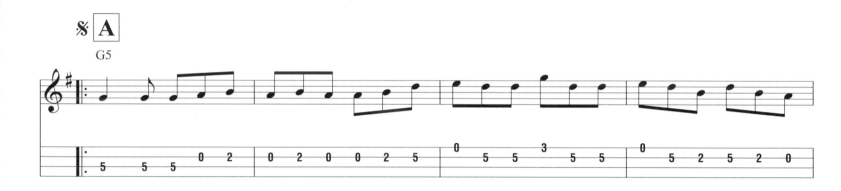

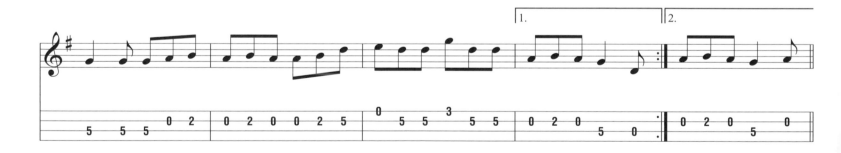

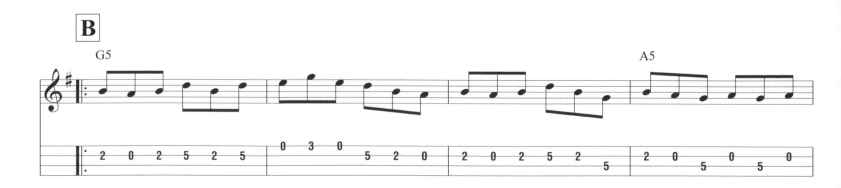

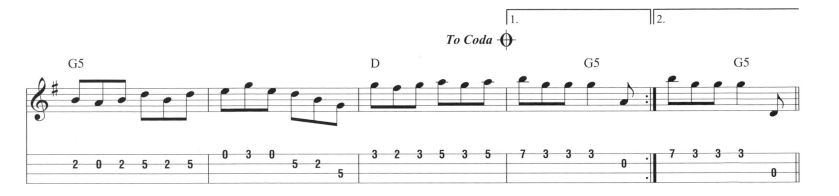

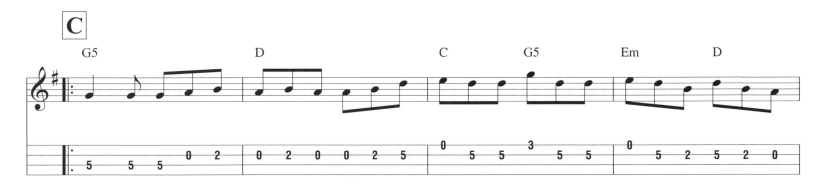

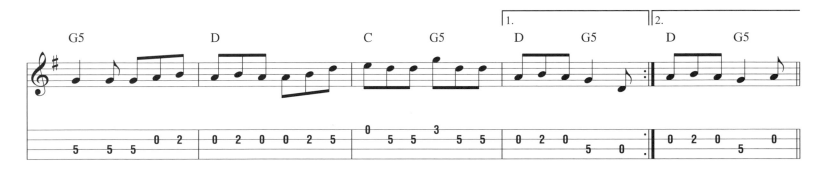

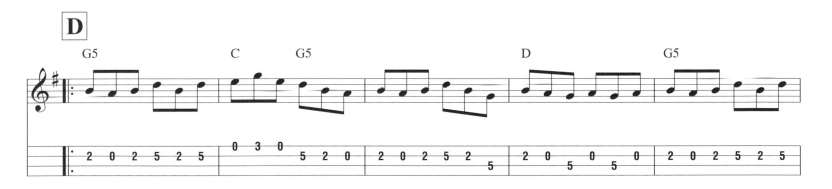

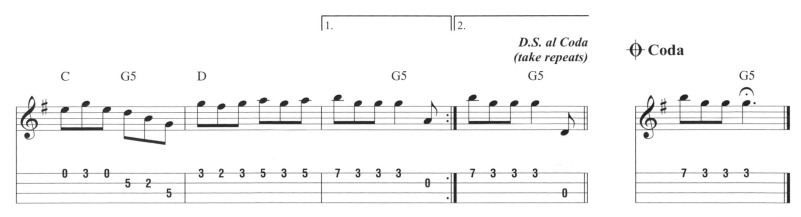

Blackbird

Words and Music by John Lennon and Paul McCartney

Interlude

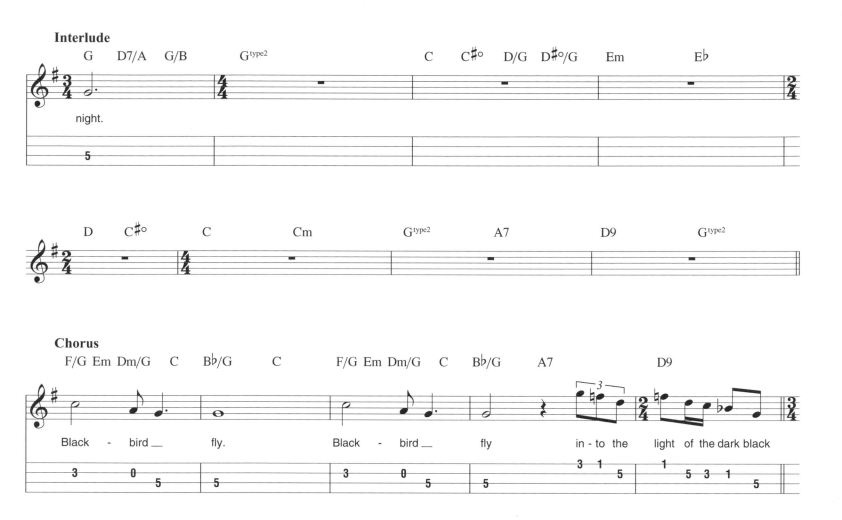

Chorus

Black - bird __ fly. Black - bird __ fly in - to the light of the dark black

Interlude

night. *rit.*

D.S. al Coda
(no repeat)

A tempo

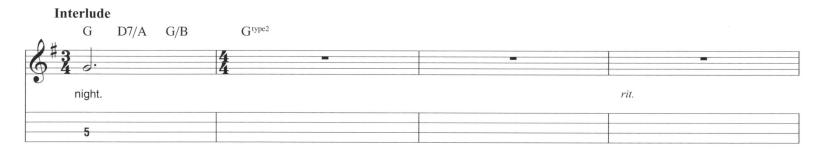

✛ **Coda**

You were on - ly wait-ing for this mo-ment to a - rise. You were on - ly wait-ing for this mo-ment to a - rise.

Hal Leonard Mandolin Play-Along Series

The Mandolin Play-Along Series will help you play your favorite songs quickly and easily. Just follow the written music, listen to the CD to hear how the mandolin should sound, and then play along using the separate backing tracks. Standard notation and tablature are both included in the book. The CD is playable on any CD player, and is also enhanced so Mac and PC users can adjust the recording to any tempo without changing the pitch!

INCLUDES TAB

1. BLUEGRASS
Angeline the Baker • Billy in the Low Ground • Blackberry Blossom • Fisher's Hornpipe • Old Joe Clark • Salt Creek • Soldier's Joy • Whiskey Before Breakfast.
00702517 Book/CD Pack..$14.99

2. CELTIC
A Fig for a Kiss • The Kesh Jig • Morrison's Jig • The Red Haired Boy • Rights of Man • Star of Munster • The Star of the County Down • Temperence Reel.
00702518 Book/CD Pack..$14.99

3. POP HITS
Brown Eyed Girl • I Shot the Sheriff • In My Life • Mrs. Robinson • Stand by Me • Superstition • Tears in Heaven • You Can't Hurry Love.
00702519 Book/CD Pack..$14.99

4. J.S. BACH
Bourree in E Minor • Invention No.1 (Bach) • Invention No.2 (Bach) • Jesu, Joy of Man's Desiring • March in D Major • Minuet in G • Musette in D Major • Sleepers, Awake (Wachet Auf).
00702520 Book/CD Pack..$14.99

5. GYPSY SWING
After You've Gone • Avalon • China Boy • Dark Eyes • Indiana (Back Home Again in Indiana) • Limehouse Blues • The Sheik of Araby • Tiger Rag (Hold That Tiger).
00702521 Book/CD Pack..$14.99

6. ROCK HITS
Back in the High Life Again • Copperhead Road • Going to California • Ho Hey • Iris • Losing My Religion • Maggie May • Sunny Came Home.
00119367 Book/CD Pack..$16.99

7. ITALIAN CLASSICS
Come Back to Sorrento • La Spagnola • Mattinata • 'O Sole Mio • Oh Marie • Santa Lucia • Tarantella • Vieni Sul Mar.
00119368 Book/CD Pack..$16.99

8. MANDOLIN FAVORITES
Arrivederci Roma (Goodbye to Rome) • The Godfather (Love Theme) • Misirlou • Never on Sunday • Over the Rainbow • Spanish Eyes • That's Amoré (That's Love) • Theme from "Zorba the Greek".
00119494 Book/CD Pack..$16.99

9. CHRISTMAS CAROLS
Angels We Have Heard on High • Carol of the Bells • Go, Tell It on the Mountain • Hark! the Herald Angels Sing • Joy to the World • O Holy Night • Silent Night • We Wish You a Merry Christmas.
00119895 Book/CD Pack..$14.99

HAL•LEONARD® CORPORATION
7777 W. BLUEMOUND RD. P.O. BOX 13819 MILWAUKEE, WI 53213

Prices, contents, and availability subject to change without notice.

www.halleonard.com

0613

Great Mandolin Publications

from

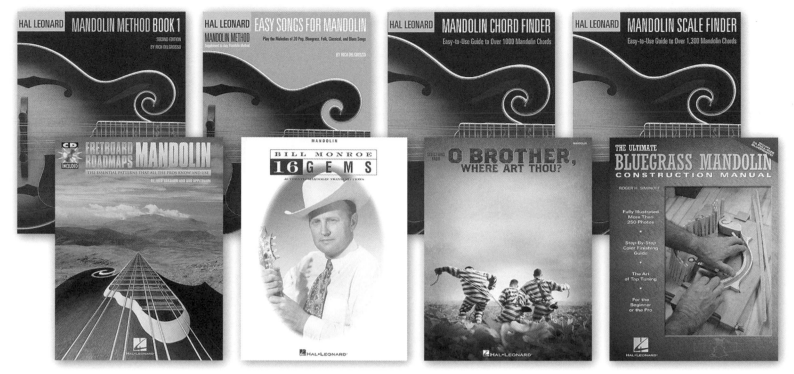

101 TIPS FROM HAL LEONARD

STUFF ALL THE PROS KNOW AND USE

Ready to take your skills to the next level? These books present valuable how-to insight that musicians of all styles and levels can benefit from. The text, photos, music, diagrams and accompanying audio provide a terrific, easy-to-use resource for a variety of topics.

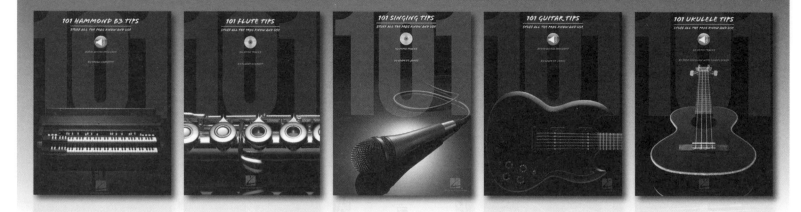

101 HAMMOND B-3 TIPS
by Brian Charette
Topics include: funky scales and modes; unconventional harmonies; creative chord voicings; cool drawbar settings; ear-grabbing special effects; professional gigging advice; practicing effectively; making good use of the pedals; and much more!
00128918 Book/Online Audio $14.99

101 HARMONICA TIPS
by Steve Cohen
Topics include: techniques, position playing, soloing, accompaniment, the blues, equipment, performance, maintenance, and much more!
00821040 Book/CD Pack...............................$16.99

101 CELLO TIPS—2ND EDITION
by Angela Schmidt
Topics include: bowing techniques, non-classical playing, electric cellos, accessories, gig tips, practicing, recording and much more!
00149094 Book/Online Audio $14.99

101 FLUTE TIPS
by Elaine Schmidt
Topics include: selecting the right flute for you, finding the right teacher, warm-up exercises, practicing effectively, taking good care of your flute, gigging advice, staying and playing healthy, and much more.
00119883 Book/CD Pack.................................$14.99

101 SAXOPHONE TIPS
by Eric Morones
Topics include: techniques; maintenance; equipment; practicing; recording; performance; and much more!
00311082 Book/CD Pack.................................$14.95

101 SINGING TIPS
by Adam St. James
Topics include: vocal exercises, breathing exercises, the singer's health, preparation, technique, understanding music, singing harmony, microphones, career advice, and much more!
00740308 Book/CD Pack.................................$14.95

101 TRUMPET TIPS
by Scott Barnard
Topics include: techniques, articulation, tone production, soloing, exercises, special effects, equipment, performance, maintenance and much more.
00312082 Book/CD Pack.................................$14.99

101 UPRIGHT BASS TIPS
by Andy McKee
Topics include: right- and left-hand technique, improvising and soloing, practicing, proper care of the instrument, ear training, performance, and much more.
00102009 Book/Online Audio $14.99

101 BASS TIPS
by Gary Willis
Topics include: techniques, improvising and soloing, equipment, practicing, ear training, performance, theory, and much more.
00695542 Book/Online Audio $16.95

101 DRUM TIPS—2ND EDITION
by Scott Schroedl
Topics include: grooves, practicing, warming up, tuning, gear, performance, and much more!
00151936 Book/Online Audio $14.99

101 FIVE-STRING BANJO TIPS
by Fred Sokolow
Topics include: techniques, ear training, performance, and much more!
00696647 Book/CD Pack.................................$14.99

101 GUITAR TIPS
by Adam St. James
Topics include: scales, music theory, truss rod adjustments, proper recording studio set-ups, and much more. The book also features snippets of advice from some of the most celebrated guitarists and producers in the music business.
00695737 Book/Online Audio $16.95

101 MANDOLIN TIPS
by Fred Sokolow
Topics include: playing tips, practicing tips, accessories, mandolin history and lore, practical music theory, and much more!
00119493 Book/Online Audio $14.99

101 RECORDING TIPS
by Adam St. James
This book contains recording tips, suggestions, and advice learned firsthand from legendary producers, engineers, and artists. These tricks of the trade will improve anyone's home or pro studio recordings.
00311035 Book/CD Pack...............................$14.95

101 UKULELE TIPS
by Fred Sokolow with Ronny Schiff
Topics include: techniques, improvising and soloing, equipment, practicing, ear training, performance, uke history and lore, and much more!
00696596 Book/Online Audio $14.99

101 VIOLIN TIPS
by Angela Schmidt
Topics include: bowing techniques, non-classical playing, electric violins, accessories, gig tips, practicing, recording, and much more!
00842672 Book/CD Pack.................................$14.99

Prices, contents and availability subject to change without notice.

HAL•LEONARD® CORPORATION
7777 W. BLUEMOUND RD. P.O. BOX 13819 MILWAUKEE, WI 53213
www.halleonard.com